NELSON

QUICKCHECK
PLACEMENT TESTS

NEW EDITION

W·S·FOWLER

NORMAN COE

Thomas Nelson and Sons Ltd
Nelson House   Mayfield Road
Walton-on-Thames   Surrey
KT12 5PL   UK

51 York Place
Edinburgh
EH1 3JD   UK

Thomas Nelson (Hong Kong) Ltd
Toppan Building 10/F
22A Westlands Road
Quarry Bay   Hong Kong

© W.S. Fowler and Norman Coe 1978, 1987
Original edition first published by Thomas Nelson and Sons Ltd 1978
This edition first published by Thomas Nelson and Sons Ltd 1987

ISBN 0-17-555563-X
NPN 9 8 7 6 5 4 3

Typeset by DP Press   Sevenoaks
Printed in the UK

Permission to copy
The material in this book is copyright. However, the publisher grants permission for copies of the pages of test papers to be made without fee as follows:

Private purchasers may make copies for use by their own students; school purchasers may make copies for use within and by the staff and students of the school only. This permission to copy does not extend to additional schools or branches of an institution, who should purchase a separate master copy of the book for their own use.

For copying in any other circumstances prior permission in writing must be obtained from Thomas Nelson and Sons Limited.

NELSON QUICKCHECK PLACEMENT TESTS
INTRODUCTION

Description
Nelson Quickcheck Placement Tests are made up of four tests of equal difficulty, designated A, B, C and D. Each test contains four sections of 25 questions, graded Elementary, Lower Intermediate, Upper Intermediate and Advanced. Students must achieve the pass score in each section before proceeding to the next. A student who qualifies for the final section will have answered 100 questions in all.

Purpose
The *Quickcheck* series, designed for rapid placement testing, has been produced from the *Nelson English Language Tests* battery in response to requests from schools that have a large number of new students to place in appropriate classes at peak times in the year. It is therefore particularly suitable on Summer School courses and for enrolment on longer courses where time is insufficient to choose an appropriate test from the *Nelson English Language Tests* on the basis of individual interviews with students. The *Quickcheck* series can nevertheless be used in conjunction with the *Nelson English Language Tests* battery if confirmation of scores obtained is required.

Content
The questions in the four *Quickcheck* tests have been carefully selected from the ten levels of the *Nelson English Language Tests* battery, which range from near-beginner level up to Cambridge Certificate of Proficiency. Questions with the highest discrimination rating were chosen in each case. The tests are in multiple-choice format, to ensure rapid marking, and consist of items measuring the recognition of correct grammatical forms and lexical choices in context. All items have been extensively pre-tested with students from a variety of first-language backgrounds.

Validity
While the tests are highly accurate and have been successfully employed in a large number of schools, we would not claim that they provide the same degree of precision in placement as the individual tests of the *Nelson English Language Tests* battery. We therefore suggest, especially in the case of general courses where the school has a large number of different levels, that the appropriate test from the battery, as indicated in Table 2, should be used for confirmation in doubtful cases.

Scoring and Administration
- Each of the four sections of a *Quickcheck* test contains 25 questions; the pass mark in order to proceed to the next section is 15.
- The test papers have been designed to be photocopied onto A4 sheets for distribution to students.
- Students should complete a page at a time in not more than 15 minutes.
- To avoid errors in marking, they should work in pencil and, if they change their minds, *erase* the incorrect answer.
- Test papers can be marked rapidly using the answer sheet mask provided.
- Students obtaining 15 or more proceed to the next section.
- Those who fail to do so can either be placed in the appropriate level, or in doubtful cases (13 or 14 correct) be asked to do the equivalent section of another *Quickcheck* test.
- If time permits, the appropriate test in the *Nelson English Language Tests* battery should be employed for greater accuracy. In such cases, however, it must be remembered that *Quickcheck* A is drawn from the corresponding *NELT* battery series, so that the test chosen from this battery must have a different letter designation to avoid repetition of items.

Security
Since scores on any one of the four *Quickcheck* tests, A, B, C and D, will be almost the same for any given section, security can be maintained among large groups of incoming students by giving different tests to those sitting next to one another.

Nelson Quickcheck Placement Tests and the Nelson English Language Tests battery

TABLE 1: *NELSON ENGLISH LANGUAGE TESTS* BATTERY LEVELS

Test	Estimated level (pass)	Relationship: international examinations
050	False beginner	
100	Lower intermediate	
150	Lower intermediate	
200	Intermediate	Enter Cambridge Preliminary class
250	Intermediate	Enter Oxford Preliminary class
300	Upper intermediate	Enter First Certificate class
350	Upper intermediate	Predicts First Certificate result
400	Advanced	Equal to First Certificate
450	Advanced	Enter Oxford Advanced class
500	Advanced	Enter Cambridge Proficiency class

- In all cases, there are 50 questions, and the pass mark is 30.
- A score of 40 or over indicates that a test two levels higher should be attempted for confirmation.
- A score of 20 or below indicates that a test two levels lower should be attempted for confirmation.
- The time for these tests is not more than 45 minutes.
- All tests can be marked with the masks provided in the *Teacher's Book*.

TABLE 2: *NELSON QUICKCHECK PLACEMENT TESTS*
Relationship with *NELT* battery and Test Procedure

Quickcheck section	Student score	Action/Confirmation
1	0–10	Pure beginner. No further testing.
	11–14	Confirm with Test 050
	15 +	Proceed to Section 2
2	0–10	Confirm with Test 100
	11–14	Confirm with Test 150
	15 +	Proceed to Section 3
3	0–10	Confirm with Test 200
	11–14	Confirm with Test 250
	15 +	Proceed to Section 4
4	0–10	Confirm with Test 300
	11–14	Confirm with Test 350
	15 +	Add up total score for four sections: Total score below 80 (confirm: Test 400) Total score 80–89 (confirm: Test 450) Total score 90 + (confirm: Test 500)

- In cases where time does not permit confirmation of results by using the *Nelson English Language Tests* battery, use these two tables as a guide to class level.

Examples:
A student scoring 12 on Section 2 (Test 150) = Lower Intermediate
A student scoring 12 on Section 3 (Test 250) could go into a class preparing for Oxford Preliminary, and should pass Cambridge Preliminary.
A student scoring 12 on Section 4 (Test 350) could go into a Cambridge First Certificate class, and would have a good chance of passing.
A student who passed all four sections with 85% is above First Certificate level and could go into a class preparing for the Oxford Advanced.

Example:

This _____ a book.
is ■ ☐ am
are ☐ ☐ be

In each question, only one of the four answers is correct. Choose the correct answer and fill in the square next to it. Fill in only one square for each question. The example shows you what to do.

A1

1 Tony is looking at _____ .
 - she ☐ ☐ he
 - her ☐ ☐ here

2 What's that girl?
 - It's a student. ☐ ☐ She's student.
 - She's a student. ☐ ☐ She's a student girl.

3 'Whose flowers are they?' 'They're _____ .'
 - to Mary ☐ ☐ of Mary
 - Maries ☐ ☐ Mary's

4
 - Sally's sister pretty and they are, too. ☐ ☐ Sally's pretty and they're too.
 - Sally's pretty and they are, too. ☐ ☐ Sally's pretty but they are.

5
 - That girl is some of my friends. ☐ ☐ This girl is one of my friends.
 - That girl is me friend. ☐ ☐ This girl's are friends.

6 Where _____ on Saturdays?
 - do go John ☐ ☐ John goes
 - does John go ☐ ☐ John does go

7
 - Go there to they. ☐ ☐ Go there to them.
 - Go here to we. ☐ ☐ Go here to us.

8 'Do you like that shop?' 'Yes, I _____ every week.'
 - come there ☐ ☐ come here
 - go there ☐ ☐ go here

9 I feel very well because I went to bed very early _____ .
 - last night ☐ ☐ tonight
 - this night ☐ ☐ in the night

10 My brother was _____ all week.
 - at the home ☐ ☐ at home
 - in the home ☐ ☐ in home

11 James _____ to play football tomorrow.
 - is going ☐ ☐ can
 - shall ☐ ☐ will

12 Jack is writing _____ .
 - with pen ☐ ☐ on paper
 - by a pen ☐ ☐ out of a pen

13 This is an old photograph of me when I _____ .
 - have short hairs ☐ ☐ had short hairs
 - have short hair ☐ ☐ had short hair

14 When we got to school, we _____ the bell.
 - heard ☐ ☐ were hearing
 - listened ☐ ☐ were listening

15 'Did you see the man on top of the church last Saturday?' 'No, why _____ '
 - was he here? ☐ ☐ has he been here?
 - was he there? ☐ ☐ has he been there?

16 This is _____ that.
 - the same as ☐ ☐ the same that
 - different that ☐ ☐ the different from

17 When _____ , give her this book.
 - Alison will arrive ☐ ☐ is Alison arriving
 - Alison arrive ☐ ☐ Alison arrives

18
 - What shoes are they made? ☐ ☐ What shoes are made of?
 - What are shoes made of? ☐ ☐ What are made of shoes?

19 _____ lovely food!
 - What ☐ ☐ Which a
 - Which ☐ ☐ What a

20 I'm going to give _____ .
 - to him a record ☐ ☐ him a record
 - a record him ☐ ☐ some record to him

21 How's the baby?
 - He's Alison's. ☐ ☐ She's very well.
 - That's the baby. ☐ ☐ She's a girl.

22 His daughter is _____ .
 - as old as yours ☐ ☐ as old as your one
 - so old as yours ☐ ☐ so old as your one

23
 - Was the French women old? ☐ ☐ Was the French women an old?
 - Were the French women some old? ☐ ☐ Were the French women old?

24 He had previously had a car but it _____ several times during the spring.
 - was breaking down ☐ ☐ was breaking up
 - had broken down ☐ ☐ had broken up

25 We _____ my cousin since last Christmas.
 - aren't seeing ☐ ☐ haven't seen
 - didn't see ☐ ☐ don't see

Name and date

Quickcheck Test **A1**

A Nelson Copy Master   © W S Fowler and Norman Coe 1987

Example:

This _____ a book.
- is ■
- am ☐
- are ☐
- be ☐

In each question, only one of the four answers is correct. Choose the correct answer and fill in the square next to it. Fill in only one square for each question. The example shows you what to do.

A2

1. There are twelve of us, so _____ get into the car at the same time.
   - we may not all ☐
   - all we may not ☐
   - we can't all ☐
   - all we can't ☐

2. Her children tell her that _____ old to drive a car.
   - she's getting so ☐
   - she gets too ☐
   - she's getting too ☐
   - she gets so ☐

3. When there's a public rocket service to the moon, her father has promised _____ her there.
   - bringing ☐
   - taking ☐
   - to bring ☐
   - to take ☐

4. _____ at the moment, I'll go to the shops.
   - As it doesn't rain ☐
   - For it doesn't rain ☐
   - As it isn't raining ☐
   - For it isn't raining ☐

5. In a shop _____ customers.
   - it is important pleasing ☐
   - it is important to please ☐
   - there is important pleasing ☐
   - there is important to please ☐

6. Your bicycle shouldn't be in the house! _____
   - Get out it! ☐
   - Put it off! ☐
   - Take it out! ☐
   - Take away it! ☐

7. He's a good guitarist, but he plays the piano _____ .
   - quiet well ☐
   - much better ☐
   - very good ☐
   - too hardly ☐

8. Molly doesn't eat fish. _____
   - John doesn't that either. ☐
   - So doesn't John. ☐
   - Neither does John. ☐
   - John doesn't too. ☐

9. She always buys _____ my birthday.
   - something awful for ☐
   - anything nice to ☐
   - something awful to ☐
   - anything nice for ☐

10. She hardly ever eats _____ potatoes.
    - neither bread nor ☐
    - bread or ☐
    - or bread or ☐
    - neither bread or ☐

11. I _____ to your letter of the 15th.
    - would like to reply ☐
    - like to reply ☐
    - am wanting to reply ☐
    - would like replying ☐

12. Your letter _____ .
    - has arrived two days ago ☐
    - arrived two days ago ☐
    - arrived since two days ☐
    - has arrived since two days ☐

13. If I _____ about it earlier I would have told you.
    - knew ☐
    - would know ☐
    - would have known ☐
    - had known ☐

14. I'll ring you as soon as I _____ there.
    - get ☐
    - shall get ☐
    - will have got ☐
    - will get ☐

15. John Marshall is a friend of mine. You _____ him last year when you were in England.
    - may meet ☐
    - can meet ☐
    - may have met ☐
    - can have met ☐

16. He didn't thank me for the present. That's _____ annoyed me.
    - what ☐
    - the which ☐
    - the thing what ☐
    - that which ☐

17. I'll have to buy _____ trousers.
    - two ☐
    - a couple of ☐
    - a ☐
    - a pair of ☐

18. She looks _____ .
    - pleasantly ☐
    - that she's pleasant ☐
    - pleasant ☐
    - to be pleasant ☐

19. I've been looking for you _____ .
    - everywhere ☐
    - for all places ☐
    - anywhere ☐
    - in all places ☐

20. Send him to the baker's _____ the bread.
    - for buying ☐
    - to buy ☐
    - in order he buys ☐
    - for to buy ☐

21. He didn't know _____ or go home.
    - if to wait ☐
    - whether to wait ☐
    - to wait ☐
    - if that he should wait ☐

22. If you _____ help you, you only have to ask me.
    - want me to ☐
    - want that I ☐
    - want I should ☐
    - are wanting me to ☐

23. 'I'm going to the theatre tonight.' 'So _____ .'
    - do I ☐
    - will I ☐
    - I will ☐
    - am I ☐

24. He wants to get a better _____ and earn more money.
    - employ ☐
    - work ☐
    - job ☐
    - employment ☐

25. I didn't hear what he was _____ .
    - speaking ☐
    - saying ☐
    - talking ☐
    - telling ☐

Name and date

Quickcheck Test A2

Example:

This _____ a book.
- is ■
- am ☐
- are ☐
- be ☐

1. I wish I _____ suggest something more suitable, but this is all we have.
   - should ☐
   - can ☐
   - could ☐
   - would ☐

2. _____ for her birthday.
   - $50 they were given to her ☐
   - She was been given $50 ☐
   - She was given $50 ☐
   - There were given to her $50 ☐

3. I _____ since breakfast and I'm very tired.
   - travel ☐
   - am travelling ☐
   - was travelling ☐
   - have been travelling ☐

4. His telegram said, 'I _____ on the 7th.'
   - will be arrive ☐
   - will be arrived ☐
   - am arriving ☐
   - would arrive ☐

5. I don't think we've met before. You're confusing me with _____ .
   - one other ☐
   - someone else ☐
   - other person ☐
   - some other ☐

6. _____ open the door for you?
   - Do you want that I ☐
   - Will I ☐
   - Shall I ☐
   - Would you like that I ☐

7. He _____ in his homework.
   - did a lot of faults ☐
   - made a lot of mistakes ☐
   - did a lot of mistakes ☐
   - made a lot of faults ☐

8. Will you be able to come to the meeting?' _____ '
   - I'm not afraid so. ☐
   - I'm sorry not. ☐
   - I'm afraid not. ☐
   - I'm sorry that 'no'. ☐

9. He was a good runner so he _____ escape from the police.
   - was able to ☐
   - succeeded to ☐
   - could ☐
   - might ☐

10. _____ a good thing they didn't catch you.
    - That's ☐
    - It's ☐
    - What's ☐
    - There's ☐

11. That's the course of studies _____ .
    - I'm interested in ☐
    - what I'm interested on ☐
    - I'm interested on ☐
    - what I'm interested in ☐

12. I would like _____ it again.
    - that you read ☐
    - you to read ☐
    - you reading ☐
    - you read ☐

13. He came to the party, _____ he hadn't been invited.
    - in case ☐
    - even ☐
    - in spite of ☐
    - although ☐

In each question, only one of the four answers is correct. Choose the correct answer and fill in the square next to it. Fill in only one square for each question. The example shows you what to do.

A3

14. He didn't take the flat because he couldn't afford the _____ .
    - rent ☐
    - hire ☐
    - salary ☐
    - fare ☐

15. He stayed under water for two minutes and then swam to the _____ .
    - sea ☐
    - level ☐
    - surface ☐
    - ground ☐

16. She was sitting _____ on the park bench.
    - by herself ☐
    - for herself ☐
    - only herself ☐
    - in her own ☐

17. We were in the station for at least half an hour, waiting _____ start.
    - for the train ☐
    - the train to ☐
    - the train's ☐
    - for the train to ☐

18. How long does the train take to _____ to London?
    - make ☐
    - reach ☐
    - get ☐
    - arrive ☐

19. Everyone in the factory has to be _____ by 8 o'clock.
    - at work ☐
    - in job ☐
    - in work ☐
    - at job ☐

20. We talked about a lot of things _____ the way to the office.
    - through ☐
    - on ☐
    - by ☐
    - in ☐

21. I _____ you before now but I've been too busy.
    - must have rung ☐
    - should have rung ☐
    - had to ring ☐
    - ought to ring ☐

22. My boss never gives me clear instructions. But you _____ the same problems with yours, too.
    - must have ☐
    - ought to have ☐
    - have to have ☐
    - can have ☐

23. Dinner will be ready _____ but we have time for a drink before then.
    - currently ☐
    - lately ☐
    - suddenly ☐
    - presently ☐

24. We have _____ for a new secretary but we haven't had any replies yet.
    - announced ☐
    - advised ☐
    - advertised ☐
    - noticed ☐

25. 100 competitors had _____ the race.
    - taken part ☐
    - entered for ☐
    - put themselves for ☐
    - put their names for ☐

Name and date

Quickcheck Test A3

A Nelson Copy Master © W S Fowler and Norman Coe 1987

Example:

This _____ a book.
- is ■
- am ☐
- are ☐
- be ☐

In each question, only one of the four answers is correct. Choose the correct answer and fill in the square next to it. Fill in only one square for each question. The example shows you what to do.

A4

1. I've _____ for the job and I hope I get it.
   - succeeded ☐
   - presented ☐
   - applied ☐
   - appointed ☐

2. I never expected you to turn _____ at the meeting. I thought you were abroad.
   - in ☐
   - around ☐
   - up ☐
   - on ☐

3. As far as he's concerned, one piece of music is very much like _____ .
   - an other ☐
   - one other ☐
   - other ☐
   - another ☐

4. She was wearing _____ beautiful clothes that I envied her.
   - a so ☐
   - so ☐
   - such ☐
   - such a ☐

5. I woke up in the middle of the night and couldn't _____ again.
   - put myself to sleep ☐
   - get back to sleep ☐
   - put myself for sleeping ☐
   - get back to sleeping ☐

6. I crossed the room and _____ a light shone through the window.
   - while doing like that ☐
   - as I did like that ☐
   - as I did so ☐
   - at doing so ☐

7. I wish I _____ on the time the film started before we came out.
   - would check ☐
   - had checked ☐
   - would have checked ☐
   - have checked ☐

8. I'll ask the waiter for the bill when you _____ your coffee.
   - will have finished ☐
   - will finish ☐
   - have finished ☐
   - shall finish ☐

9. There was a suitcase _____ mine on the luggage rack.
   - like ☐
   - as ☐
   - similar than ☐
   - the same that ☐

10. He _____ out of the window for a moment and then went on working.
    - regarded ☐
    - glanced ☐
    - viewed ☐
    - glimpsed ☐

11. I'd like to take _____ of this opportunity to thank you all for your co-operation.
    - advantage ☐
    - occasion ☐
    - benefit ☐
    - profit ☐

12. Our main concern is to raise the voters' _____ of living.
    - condition ☐
    - standard ☐
    - capacity ☐
    - degree ☐

13. For heaven's _____ don't make a noise.
    - behalf ☐
    - reason ☐
    - love ☐
    - sake ☐

14. He reminds me _____ someone I knew in the army.
    - of ☐
    - to ☐
    - from ☐
    - with ☐

15. He was _____ that he called the doctor.
    - having such ache ☐
    - in such ache ☐
    - in such pain ☐
    - with such pain ☐

16. I daren't _____ to upset her.
    - do anything ☐
    - to do something ☐
    - do nothing ☐
    - to do a thing ☐

17. We've _____ sugar. Ask Mrs Jones to lend us some.
    - run away with ☐
    - run down ☐
    - run off ☐
    - run out of ☐

18. I _____ you that the goods will be delivered next week.
    - confirm ☐
    - undergo ☐
    - assure ☐
    - insist ☐

19. The Second World War _____ in 1939.
    - broke out ☐
    - broke open ☐
    - broke up ☐
    - broke off ☐

20. We can never relax in this office. New problems are continually _____ .
    - coming out ☐
    - coming up ☐
    - raising ☐
    - presenting ☐

21. This test _____ a number of multiple-choice questions.
    - composes of ☐
    - consists of ☐
    - composes in ☐
    - consists in ☐

22. Hot metal _____ as it grows cooler.
    - contracts ☐
    - compresses ☐
    - reduces ☐
    - condenses ☐

23. He thinks about nothing but playing golf. He's completely _____ to it.
    - overcome ☐
    - ascribed ☐
    - tempted ☐
    - addicted ☐

24. He's always _____ the Government but he never votes in the elections.
    - running out ☐
    - calling off ☐
    - running down ☐
    - calling out ☐

25. I'm sorry to _____ you while you're working but I must ask you a question.
    - molest ☐
    - bother ☐
    - interfere ☐
    - intrude ☐

Name and date

Quickcheck Test A4

A Nelson Copy Master © W S Fowler and Norman Coe 1987

In each question, only one of the four answers is correct. Choose the correct answer and fill in the square next to it. Fill in only one square for each question. The example shows you what to do.

Example:

This _____ a book.
is ■   am ☐
are ☐   be ☐

B1

1 Mary speaks English, but _____

speaks Bill? ☐   Bill speaks? ☐
does Bill? ☐   Bill does? ☐

2 Do you draw or sing?

I'm drawing and singing. ☐   I draw and I sing. ☐
I do draw and singing. ☐   I drawing and singing. ☐

3 Ken's behind Mary. Mary's _____ Ken.

in front of ☐   beside ☐
between ☐   next ☐

4 Monday is the first day.

Tuesday is the fourth. ☐   The second is thursday. ☐
The second is tuesday. ☐   Thursday is the fourth. ☐

5

Look my garden, Susan! ☐   Susan looks my garden. ☐
Look at my garden, Susan! ☐   Susan is look at my garden. ☐

6 'Whose is this house?' 'It's _____.'

our ☐   our one ☐
ours ☐   ours one ☐

7 Are the bicycles in the garage? 'No, there _____ in the garage.'

is anything ☐   isn't nothing ☐
isn't something ☐   is nothing ☐

8 Pat's a girl _____ long arms.

with some ☐   with ☐
with her ☐   with the ☐

9 What time _____ dinner?

does Peter have ☐   do Peter has ☐
does Peter has ☐   Peter has ☐

10 Her father will come at 8 o'clock _____.

in this afternoon ☐   this afternoon ☐
in this evening ☐   this evening ☐

11 Nancy works in a shop and _____.

that does Alan too ☐   so does Alan too ☐
so Alan too does ☐   that Alan too does ☐

12 What is your cousin?

That's she. ☐   This is her. ☐
I haven't got any. ☐   She's a doctor. ☐

13 What _____ on Saturday?

does John usually do ☐   John usually does ☐
usually does John ☐   does John usually ☐

14 They told _____ next week.

him coming back ☐   to him come back ☐
him to come back ☐   he could come back ☐

15 My youngest daughter _____ late for school.

is never coming ☐   never is coming ☐
comes never ☐   has never been ☐

16 Have you ever been to Ireland?

Not already. ☐   Not ever. ☐
Not yet. ☐   Not still. ☐

17 'Shall I get anything for you at the shop?' 'Yes, _____ apples.'

bring a little ☐   take a few ☐
take any ☐   bring some ☐

18 _____ clever idea!

What ☐   What a ☐
So ☐   How ☐

19 _____ to get rich.

Not every young man try ☐   No every young man try ☐
Not every young man tries ☐   No every young man tries ☐

20 How's John's sister?

This is her. ☐   She's fine. ☐
That's she. ☐   She's good. ☐

21 Why have you _____ to me?

gone ☐   came ☐
come ☐   went ☐

22 Last Sunday _____ thousands of people on the beach.

it was ☐   there were ☐
there was ☐   they were ☐

23

Was the big car expensive? ☐   Was the expensive car a big? ☐
Was expensive the big car? ☐   Was the expensive a big car? ☐

24 'In the future scientists _____ a lot of money,' his parents said.

shall earn ☐   will earn ☐
going to earn ☐   are earning ☐

25 I passed my exams but it was a long time _____ my friends about it.

that I didn't tell ☐   before I told ☐
when I wasn't telling ☐   before telling ☐

Name and date

Quickcheck Test B1

In each question, only one of the four answers is correct. Choose the correct answer and fill in the square next to it. Fill in only one square for each question. The example shows you what to do.

Example:

This _____ a book.		
is ■	am ☐	
are ☐	be ☐	

B2

1 'The best _____ now is to write to her,' my friend said.

    thing that you do ☐   ☑ you should do
    thing to do ☐   ☐ to do

2 Mrs Penfield telephoned early last Saturday while I _____ bed.

    still was in the ☐   ☐ was still in
    still was in ☐   ☐ was still in the

3 Jim was _____ he forgot his books.

    so excited that ☐   ☐ so much excited
    so excited as ☐   ☐ so excited than

4 Is her _____ than mine?

    shorter hair ☐   ☐ more short hair
    hair more short ☐   ☐ hair shorter

5 Phone me when you get _____ .

    in home ☐   ☐ to home
    home ☐   ☐ at home

6 The baby is crying! Will you _____ while I prepare his milk?

    make him up ☐   ☐ tear him up
    look after him ☐   ☐ care him

7 To travel from England to Scotland you _____ a passport.

    haven't got ☐   ☐ mustn't have
    needn't ☐   ☐ don't need

8 I _____ home at half past six.

    come at ☐   ☐ get
    arrive in ☐   ☐ go to

9 I _____ meet her every day.

    used to ☑   ☐ am not able
    liked ☐   ☐ wanted

10 Tell _____ back tomorrow.

    Pam come ☐   ☐ to Pam to come
    to Pam come ☐   ☐ Pam to come

11 Don't you remember that we _____ to the cinema tonight?

    will be gone ☐   ☐ are going
    would go ☐   ☐ go

12

    I'm here since half an hour. ☐   ☐ I've been here since half an hour.
    It's half an hour I am here. ☐   ☐ I've been here for half an hour.

13

    Ida had been given some money. ☐   ☐ They had been given some money to Ida.
    To Ida some money had been given. ☐   ☐ Some money to Ida had been given.

14 We went out to dinner before _____ to the cinema.

    we were going ☐   ☐ go
    going ☐   ☐ to go

15 By the time we arrive, the film _____ .

    shall have started ☐   ☐ has started
    has to start ☐   ☐ will have started

16 Would you like some more coffee? There's still _____ left.

    a few ☐   ☐ little
    a little ☐   ☐ few

17 He didn't mind _____ late because he enjoyed it.

    to work ☐   ☐ work
    that he work ☐   ☐ working

18 He asked me _____ stay.

    how long was I going to ☐   ☐ how long I was going to
    how long time I was going to ☐   ☐ how long time was I going to

19 That's the hotel _____ last year.

    where we stayed at ☐   ☐ which we stayed
    where we stayed ☐   ☐ at which we stayed at

20 She broke a _____ while she was washing up.

    glass for wine ☐   ☐ wine glass
    glass wine ☐   ☐ glass of wine

21 I'm going to the hairdresser's _____ .

    for to cut me my hair ☐   ☐ to have cut my hair
    to have my hair cut ☐   ☐ to cut my hair

22 He couldn't help _____ that his wife was worried.

    to notice ☐   ☐ noticing
    except notice ☐   ☐ notice

23 Your parents are _____ to ring the police if they don't know where you are.

    likely ☐   ☐ probably
    probable ☐   ☐ possible

24 She _____ the cups and some of them broke.

    let ☐   ☐ dropped
    let fall ☐   ☐ fell

25 He got a job in a furniture _____ .

    industry ☐   ☐ factory
    society ☐   ☐ fabric

Name and date

Quickcheck Test B2

In each question, only one of the four answers is correct. Choose the correct answer and fill in the square next to it. Fill in only one square for each question. The example shows you what to do.

Example:

This _____ a book.		
is ■	am ☐	
are ☐	be ☐	

B3

1 I was surprised my wife was out. 'She _____ shopping,' I thought.

must be gone ☐ ☐ should go
must have gone ☐ ☐ ought to have gone

2 '_____ you give me a room for the night?' I asked, on arriving at the hotel.

Should ☐ ☐ Can
Might ☐ ☐ May

3 Before _____ hope, let's try this one.

giving up ☐ ☐ to give up
taking up ☐ ☐ to take up

4 'I wonder why they're late.' 'They _____ the train.'

can have missed ☐ ☐ could miss
might miss ☐ ☐ may have missed

5 Her opinion is the same _____ her mother's.

that ☐ ☐ than
as ☐ ☐ like

6 _____ I need is a drink.

The thing what ☐ ☐ That
What ☐ ☐ The which

7 I met him _____ the stairs as I was coming up.

along ☐ ☐ for
in ☐ ☐ on

8 _____ a pity I didn't see you.

What's ☐ ☐ It's
There's ☐ ☐ That's

9 He was _____ tired to go on.

too ☐ ☐ too much
so much ☐ ☐ so

10 He _____ live in the country than in the city.

prefers ☐ ☐ likes better to
had better ☐ ☐ would rather

11 That's the dog _____ .

what we've been looking after ☐ ☐ we've been looking after
we've been after looking ☐ ☐ after which we've been looking

12 I work _____ I can.

as hardly as ☐ ☐ so hardly as
so hard as ☐ ☒ as hard as

13 'I missed the train home last night.' 'So _____ .'

did I ☐ ☐ I did
I have ☐ ☐ have I

14 He broke the world _____ for the 100 metres.

mark ☐ ☐ level
record ☐ ☐ standard

15 There are a lot of mistakes in this exercise. I'll have to _____ it again with you.

repass ☐ ☐ instruct
come through ☐ ☐ go over

16 He _____ doesn't believe it even though we've shown him the evidence.

yet ☐ ☐ already
still ☐ ☐ no longer

17 I was so tired that I would have slept _____ .

somewhere ☐ ☐ however
in whatever place ☐ ☐ anywhere

18 Every old house has _____ strange stories.

their ☐ ☐ its
his ☐ ☐ the

19 When we arrived at the hotel we asked them _____ have.

what room we may ☐ ☐ which room could we
which room we could ☐ ☐ what room could we

20 They offered _____ Number 7.

to us room ☐ ☐ us room
us the room ☐ ☐ to us the room

21 The petrol tank's empty. I _____ it up before we left home.

had to fill ☐ ☐ would have filled
should have filled ☐ ☐ must have filled

22 If only I _____ about it before we set out!

knew ☐ ☐ had known
would have known ☐ ☐ have known

23 I don't want to go into the sea. I'd rather lie on the _____ .

beach ☐ ☐ seaside
coast ☐ ☐ bank

24 I'm _____ I didn't pass the examination but I'll do better next time.

disillusioned ☐ ☐ disappointed
despaired ☐ ☐ deceived

25 I can't give you an answer yet. I'd like _____ more time to consider my decision.

fairly ☐ ☐ rather
quite ☐ ☐ hardly

Name and date

A Nelson Copy Master   © W S Fowler and Norman Coe 1987

Quickcheck Test B3

In each question, only one of the four answers is correct. Choose the correct answer and fill in the square next to it. Fill in only one square for each question. The example shows you what to do.

Example: This _____ a book.
is ■   am ☐
are ☐   be ☐

B4

1 PTO stands _____ 'Please turn over'—the page, of course.
   as ☐   like ☐
   for ☐   by ☐

2 I'll call _____ you at 8.30 and give you a lift to work.
   to ☐   for ☐
   at ☐   on ☐

3 She was very generous, _____ her efforts to save.
   in spite of ☐   nevertheless ☐
   although ☐   however ☐

4 There was no sign of panic, excitement _____ violence.
   neither ☐   nor ☐
   but ☐   or ☐

5 He is normally _____ in any emergency.
   enough calm ☐   so calmly ☐
   calm enough ☐   just calmly ☐

6 If you _____ such a long time to get dressed, we'd have arrived by now.
   wouldn't have taken ☐   wouldn't take ☐
   hadn't taken ☐   haven't taken ☐

7 'You realise that you were driving at 100 mph, don't you?' 'No, officer, I _____. This car can't do more than 80.'
   didn't need to be ☐   may not have been ☐
   needn't have been ☐   couldn't have been ☐

8 He _____ someone I knew in the army.
   remembers ☐   reminds me of ☐
   remembers me of ☐   reminds me to ☐

9 _____ in the room.
   There wasn't much furniture ☐   There weren't many furnitures ☐
   It wasn't much furniture ☐   They weren't many furnitures ☐

10 She's bought some lovely _____ to make herself a dress.
   costume ☐   pattern ☐
   clothing ☐   material ☐

11 The meeting _____ at midnight and we all went home.
   stopped up ☐   broke up ☐
   broke through ☐   stopped off ☐

12 He's not as honest as he _____.
   gives over ☐   gives away ☐
   makes up ☐   makes out ☐

13 She waited for the sound that had woken her _____.
   to be repeated ☐   to reproduce ☐
   to be recurred ☐   to revise ☐

14 He aimed his gun _____ the target.
   to ☐   in ☐
   at ☐   on ☐

15 She would have spoken if he had not _____ his hand for silence.
   risen ☐   got up ☐
   rose ☐   raised ☐

16 He looked up at the house as if he _____ how to get in.
   would wander ☐   was wandering ☐
   was wondering ☐   would wonder ☐

17 I enjoyed that dish very much. Would you mind letting me have the _____ for it?
   prescription ☐   receipt ☐
   menu ☐   recipe ☐

18 Drive carefully because there are a lot of _____ in the road.
   crosses ☐   bends ☐
   curls ☐   folds ☐

19 I didn't realise you wanted to keep the letter. I've _____ it up.
   broken ☐   pulled ☐
   torn ☐   smashed ☐

20 He _____ his engagement just before the wedding.
   broke out of ☐   broke off ☐
   broke away from ☐   broke up ☐

21 The shepherd trained the dog to look after his _____ of sheep.
   herd ☐   pack ☐
   flock ☐   collection ☐

22 The lawyer will _____ the contract for you.
   do up ☐   draw up ☐
   draw out ☐   do out ☐

23 That door _____ when you open it. You must put some oil on the hinges.
   creaks ☐   cracks ☐
   rumbles ☐   rustles ☐

24 He was _____ of deciding anything for himself.
   unable ☐   incapable ☐
   ineffective ☐   incompetent ☐

25 It would be _____ a risk to let the child go to school by himself.
   carrying ☐   running ☐
   following ☐   passing ☐

Name and date

Quickcheck Test **B4**

A Nelson Copy Master   © W S Fowler and Norman Coe 1987

In each question, only one of the four answers is correct. Choose the correct answer and fill in the square next to it. Fill in only one square for each question. The example shows you what to do.

Example: This _____ a book.
is ■ □ am
are □ □ be

C1

1 Tom is Mrs Black's son.
She is his daughter. □ □ He is her son.
She is her son. □ □ He is his son.

2
A old woman lives near me. □ □ A young woman live near my house.
An old women lives near my house. □ □ The old woman lives near me.

3 Listen to _____ sister!
she and she's □ □ her and her
her and she □ □ she and her

4
This is two lessons. □ □ This is second lesson.
These are lessons, too. □ □ This is lesson the second.

5
Pat can to have Jims' hat. □ □ Pat can to have Jim's hat.
Pat can have Jims' hat. □ □ Pat can have Jim's hat.

6 _____ the room!
Don't going to □ □ Don't go into
Not to go in □ □ Not go into

7 Lynn _____ television every evening.
watches □ □ locks
washes □ □ looks

8 Pat and Jane are _____ her.
as clever as □ □ clever that
clever than □ □ so clever as

9
What age has she? □ □ How old is she?
How many years has she? □ □ How old she is?

10 There wasn't _____ in the garden.
some people □ □ any people
anybody □ □ no persons

11 Bob's _____ .
shorter that I'm □ □ the shorter than me
the shorter than they □ □ shorter than them

12 'Are the papers in your room?' 'Yes, my mother _____ yesterday.'
put them there □ □ puts them there
put it there □ □ puts it there

13 Last year _____ to Canada.
went Mary □ □ did Mary go
Mary was □ □ Mary went

14 Last summer I taught _____ a bicycle.
to my cousin ride □ □ my cousin riding
my cousin ride □ □ my cousin to ride

15 Jill, what _____ tomorrow evening?
will you to do □ □ are you going do
are you doing □ □ do you

16 When _____ his homework?
Tom usually does □ □ does Tom usually
usually does Tom □ □ does Tom usually do

17 I spoke to _____ people at the bus-stop.
a few □ □ a pair
much □ □ another

18 What sort of car shall I get?
Get no English! □ □ Get none English!
Don't get any one English! □ □ Don't get an English one!

19 _____ these girls do you know?
Which of □ □ Who are
What of □ □ How many

20 Yesterday John _____ the bus.
waited for ten minutes □ □ was expecting ten minutes
expected for ten minutes □ □ waited ten minutes for

21 Mary bought _____ .
to Peter a pen □ □ a pen for Peter
for Peter a pen □ □ a pen to Peter

22 _____ work on Saturdays.
Sometimes I didn't □ □ Sometimes didn't I
Never didn't I □ □ Never I didn't

23 How many times have you been?
One times. □ □ Twice.
Two months. □ □ Quite much.

24 It's five months _____ to our new house.
since we moved □ □ since then we moved
that we moved us □ □ that we move

25 Hello, Janice! Tell me what _____ here today.
do you do □ □ you do
you're doing □ □ takes you

Name and date

Quickcheck Test C1

A Nelson Copy Master © W S Fowler and Norman Coe 1987

In each question, only one of the four answers is correct. Choose the correct answer and fill in the square next to it. Fill in only one square for each question. The example shows you what to do.

Example: This _____ a book.
is ■   am □
are □   be □

C2

1 A dog ran in front of my mother's car and she _____ stop very quickly.
  ought to □   had to □
  must □   had better □

2 I didn't see any animals. I don't think _____ in that park.
  they were any □   there were any ones □
  they were any ones □   there were any □

3 My mother usually has _____ bed.
  the breakfast in □   breakfast in □
  the breakfast in the □   breakfast in the □

4 The girl _____ mother was ill was crying.
  which □   of which □
  whose □   of whom □

5 I have a _____ paper in my desk.
  loss □   little of □
  lot □   little □

6 'Can't you read?' Mary said, _____ to the notice.
  and angrily pointing □   pointing angrily □
  angrily pointed □   and pointed angry □

7 It's dark without the lights. Let's _____ .
  turn them on □   to switch them on □
  switch on them □   to turn on them □

8 Everybody _____ in bed.
  has to spend some time □   have to spend sometimes □
  has to spend sometimes □   have to spend some time □

9 I've thrown away my old trousers. I'll have to buy _____ .
  a new one □   a new pair □
  some new □   some new pair □

10 Kim and Tony weren't the only people in the garden. There _____ .
  was someone more □   was another □
  were some others □   were some other ones □

11 If I had closed the window, the thief _____ .
  would not get in □   had not got in □
  has not got in □   would not have got in □

12 I've been told to investigate, so I _____ ask you some questions.
  want to □   am wanting to □
  would □   would to □

13 How _____ ?
  was the thief getting in □   the thief got in □
  has the thief got in □   did the thief get in □

14 If people _____ their houses properly, the police wouldn't have so much work to do.
  should look after □   have looked after □
  looks after □   looked after □

15 I rang him up before _____ for Rome.
  to leave □   to go out □
  leaving □   leave □

16 Ask him to go to the post office _____ some stamps.
  that he gets □   for getting □
  in order he gets □   to get □

17 She cut the cloth with _____ scissors.
  a pair of □   a couple of □
  two □   a □

18 The children _____ play with them.
  are wanting that I □   want that I □
  want me for □   want me to □

19 John is _____ .
  a friend of mine □   one friend of mine □
  a friend mine □   a friend of me □

20 She's going to the photographer's _____ .
  to have taken her photograph □   to take her photograph □
  that he takes her photograph □   to have her photograph taken □

21 _____ of them knew about the plan because it was secret.
  Some □   None □
  No one □   Any □

22 Mont Blanc, _____ we visited last summer, is the highest mountain in Europe.
  which □   where □
  what □   that □

23 This question is _____ difficult for me.
  so much □   too □
  too much □   enough □

24 Good _____ ! I hope you win the race.
  luck □   sort □
  wish □   chance □

25 Look what Father _____ me when he came home from work.
  fetched □   carried □
  brought □   took □

Name and date

A Nelson Copy Master   © W S Fowler and Norman Coe 1987

Quickcheck Test C2

In each question, only one of the four answers is correct. Choose the correct answer and fill in the square next to it. Fill in only one square for each question. The example shows you what to do.

Example:

This _____ a book.	
is ■	am ☐
are ☐	be ☐

C3

1 'Why haven't they arrived?' 'They _____ the plane.'

can have lost ☐	may have missed ☐
may have lost ☐	can have missed ☐

2 Where's the letter they wrote? _____ it?

Do you already have ☐	Do you yet have ☐
Have you yet got ☐	Have you still got ☐

3 We _____ us at 10 o'clock.

would like that you find ☐	would like you to meet ☐
want that you look for ☐	want you to wait ☐

4 I _____ this letter around for days without looking at it.

carry ☐	must carry ☐
have been carrying ☐	am carryng ☐

5 _____ entering the hall, he found everyone waiting for him.

With ☐	In ☐
At ☐	On ☐

6 _____ an empty seat at the back of the bus.

She happened to meet ☐	She happened to find ☐
It happened her she found ☐	It happened her that she met ☐

7 I don't like _____ at me.

them shouting ☐	their shout ☐
that they shout ☐	them shout ☐

8 It often snows _____ January.

in ☐	for ☐
at ☐	on ☐

9 She's been very kind, _____ ?

doesn't she ☐	hasn't she ☐
wasn't she ☐	isn't she ☐

10 He was left alone, with _____ to look after him.

someone ☐	anyone ☐
no one ☐	not one ☐

11 He _____ lives in the house where he was born.

ever ☐	already ☐
yet ☐	still ☐

12 He arrived late, _____ was annoying.

which ☐	the which ☐
what ☐	that ☐

13 They live _____ the other side of the road.

in ☐	by ☐
for ☐	on ☐

14 I've often _____ at this hotel.

remained ☐	rested ☐
passed ☐	stayed ☐

15 Your work has been _____ so we're going to give you a rise in salary.

regular ☐	well ☐
satisfactory ☐	available ☐

16 It _____ her.

is ages that I didn't see ☐	makes ages that I didn't see ☐
make ages since I saw ☐	is ages since I saw ☐

17 We had _____ hard time trying to persuade him that we gave up.

such a ☐	a so ☐
such ☐	so ☐

18 _____ they argued, the more difficult it became.

The most ☐	For how much ☐
How much ☐	The more ☐

19 I used to go to a school _____ from home.

five miles away ☐	five miles far ☐
at five miles ☐	five miles long ☐

20 He _____ for half an hour.

made us waiting ☐	made us to wait ☐
kept us to wait ☐	kept us waiting ☐

21 Would you mind _____ me a favour?

making ☐	doing ☐
to make ☐	to do ☐

22 When I _____ there I won't be able to get in.

get ☐	will get ☐
shall get ☐	am getting ☐

23 They have put the bird in a cage to _____ it from flying away.

avoid ☐	prevent ☐
resist ☐	hinder ☐

24 The _____ outside the house said 'Private'.

notice ☐	label ☐
advice ☐	signal ☐

25 I _____ an answer to my letter within a few days.

wait ☐	look forward ☐
expect ☐	hope ☐

Name and date

Quickcheck Test C3

A Nelson Copy Master   © W S Fowler and Norman Coe 1987

In each question, only one of the four answers is correct. Choose the correct answer and fill in the square next to it. Fill in only one square for each question. The example shows you what to do.

Example:

	This _____ a book.
is ■	am ☐
are ☐	be ☐

C4

1. If you don't know how to spell a word, look it _____ in the dictionary.
   - for ☐
   - up ☐
   - after ☐
   - out ☐

2. He carries _____ as if he were the boss.
   - through ☐
   - off ☐
   - out ☐
   - on ☐

3. He went on working without _____.
   - saying nothing ☐
   - saying anything ☐
   - telling anything ☐
   - telling nothing ☐

4. Everyone expected him to win but you never _____.
   - may be secure ☐
   - can learn ☐
   - can be sure ☐
   - might know ☐

5. It was difficult to _____ in the photograph because it had been taken from so far away.
   - pick her up ☐
   - take hold of her ☐
   - see through her ☐
   - make her out ☐

6. She didn't want to buy it, _____.
   - however good was it ☐
   - however good it was ☐
   - for how good might it be ☐
   - for how good it might be ☐

7. He took no notice, _____ the whole town was full of rumours.
   - although ☐
   - in spite ☐
   - however ☐
   - nevertheless ☐

8. You _____ the washing-up. I would have done it for you.
   - needn't have done ☐
   - couldn't have done ☐
   - hadn't to do ☐
   - mustn't have done ☐

9. It's a pity you've had to wait, Sir. Now _____ see if we can solve your problem?
   - let's to ☐
   - shall we ☐
   - will we ☐
   - are we going to ☐

10. She chose some very pretty _____ paper for the present.
    - packing ☐
    - covering ☐
    - wrapping ☐
    - involving ☐

11. It gave me a strange feeling of excitement to see my name _____.
    - in publication ☐
    - in press ☐
    - in news ☐
    - in print ☐

12. You'd better add it up. I'm no good at _____.
    - figures ☐
    - summaries ☐
    - counters ☐
    - characters ☐

13. Towards the top of the mountain the cliff was easier to climb, though _____ steeper.
    - hardly ☐
    - quite ☐
    - fairly ☐
    - rather ☐

14. We found little snow there, as most of it seemed _____ blown off the mountain.
    - it was ☐
    - to be ☐
    - that it had ☐
    - to have been ☐

15. We _____ the approach of the storm, but we were too busy.
    - had to notice ☐
    - must have noticed ☐
    - ought to have noticed ☑
    - should notice ☐

16. Trying to climb the mountain in such terrible conditions was _____.
    - out of touch ☐
    - beyond the reach ☐
    - off the point ☐
    - out of the question ☐

17. He'll _____ his nervousness once he's on stage.
    - get over ☐
    - get through ☐
    - get away ☐
    - get off ☐

18. There are several landladies approved by the university who take in _____.
    - residents ☐
    - inhabitants ☐
    - settlers ☐
    - lodgers ☐

19. He shook hands with his _____ before the match.
    - opponent ☐
    - competitor ☐
    - opposition ☐
    - contestant ☐

20. He has been _____ of murdering his wife.
    - charged ☐
    - blamed ☐
    - arrested ☐
    - accused ☑

21. We'll _____ you as soon as we have any further information.
    - communicate ☐
    - notify ☑
    - relate ☐
    - make known ☐

22. She's very pretty but that kind of face doesn't _____ to me.
    - appeal ☐
    - fancy ☐
    - attract ☐
    - call ☐

23. She made it _____ that she didn't approve by throwing something at me.
    - sincere ☐
    - plain ☐
    - frank ☐
    - revealed ☐

24. I put the milk _____ back in the fridge.
    - jug ☐
    - holder ☐
    - flask ☐
    - vase ☐

25. I caught a _____ of the car before it disappeared around the bend.
    - gleam ☐
    - glance ☐
    - glimpse ☐
    - glare ☐

Name and date

Quickcheck Test **C4**

A Nelson Copy Master © W S Fowler and Norman Coe 1987

Example: This _____ a book.
- is ■
- am ☐
- are ☐
- be ☐

In each question, only one of the four answers is correct. Choose the correct answer and fill in the square next to it. Fill in only one square for each question. The example shows you what to do.

D1

1. Who's that man?
   - He's teacher. ☐
   - It's John. ☐
   - Is Peter. ☐
   - That's a man. ☐

2. Mike is looking at _____ .
   - they ☐
   - she ☐
   - my ☐
   - us ☐

3.
   - Come here to my! ☐
   - Come there to we! ☐
   - Come here to us! ☐
   - Go here to us! ☐

4.
   - Jack listen my radio. ☐
   - Listen my radio, Jack! ☐
   - Jack is listen to my radio. ☐
   - Listen to my radio, Jack! ☐

5. Mary _____ play tomorrow.
   - going to ☐
   - can to ☐
   - can ☐
   - is going ☐

6. _____ live in the town.
   - Some people ☐
   - Anybody ☐
   - Somebody ☐
   - Any people ☐

7. Molly hasn't got your money. Jack hasn't got _____ .
   - it, too ☐
   - them, too ☐
   - them, either ☐
   - it, either ☐

8. Mary's here. She's just _____ .
   - come ☐
   - been ☐
   - got ☐
   - gone ☐

9. What is Peter like? He _____ .
   - is very well ☐
   - is liking tennis ☐
   - like football ☐
   - is very nice ☐

10. 'Has Jimmy got his books now?' 'Yes, my brother _____ yesterday.'
    - gave them to him ☐
    - gave to him them ☐
    - has given them to him ☐
    - has given to him them ☐

11. You can't see the sun _____ .
    - at the night ☐
    - at night ☐
    - at the nights ☐
    - at nights ☐

12. 'Have you visited Edinburgh?' '_____'
    - Not yet. ☐
    - Not ever. ☐
    - Already. ☐
    - Ever. ☐

13. Donald _____ sixteen tomorrow.
    - will be ☐
    - going to be ☐
    - shall be ☐
    - is being ☐

14. They didn't have any books that she _____ .
    - was happy ☐
    - was interested ☐
    - pleased ☐
    - liked ☐

15. Last year Mary asked me what she _____ buy me for Christmas.
    - could ☐
    - was able to ☐
    - may ☐
    - can ☐

16. There isn't _____ in the garden.
    - no person ☐
    - anyone ☐
    - persons ☐
    - any people ☐

17. He thinks John _____ .
    - the same as I ☐
    - is same as me ☐
    - is the same as me ☐
    - is the same I am ☐

18. Cathie has read _____ French books.
    - so much ☐
    - every ☐
    - the more ☐
    - a few ☐

19. Is Chris _____ Kate?
    - taller that ☐
    - so tall as ☐
    - taller ☐
    - as tall as ☐

20. It was raining when Mary _____ the bus.
    - waited ☐
    - expected ☐
    - was waiting for ☐
    - was expecting ☐

21. Was the _____ ? No, it was green.
    - big book brown ☐
    - brown book a big ☐
    - big brown book ☐
    - brown a big book ☐

22. 'Have you ever been to Scotland?' 'Yes, I _____ last year.'
    - was ☐
    - went ☐
    - have gone ☐
    - was being ☐

23. How's the old man?
    - He's sixty-five. ☐
    - That's him. ☐
    - He's much better. ☐
    - Mr Smith is the old man. ☐

24. Last week John _____ his leg.
    - fell and broke ☐
    - felt and broken ☐
    - feels and breaks ☐
    - fallen and broken ☐

25. When she asked me I _____ a few days to think about it.
    - explained her I liked ☐
    - explained her I'd like ☐
    - told her I'd like ☐
    - told her I liked ☐

Name and date

Quickcheck Test D1

A Nelson Copy Master © W S Fowler and Norman Coe 1987

Example:

This _____ a book.
is ■ □ am
are □ □ be

In each question, only one of the four answers is correct. Choose the correct answer and fill in the square next to it. Fill in only one square for each question. The example shows you what to do.

D2

1 They asked the secretary _____ them the papers.
   please to give □ □ to give
   that she give □ □ please give

2 We invited him last week but he _____ .
   didn't yet say that yes □ □ didn't yet say yes
   hasn't yet said that yes □ □ hasn't said yes yet

3 'I agree,' I said. 'I hoped _____ ,' she replied.
   that you agreed □ □ you to agree
   that you'd agree □ □ for you to agree

4 Who was the first person _____ today?
   you spoke □ □ spoke to you
   whom you spoke □ □ you spoke to

5 Jane had _____ furniture for her room.
   all □ □ many
   enough □ □ any

6 I like _____ two records.
   both these □ □ these all
   these both □ □ all these

7 _____ people came than I expected.
   Other □ □ Another
   Few □ □ Fewer

8 Simon _____ the club.
   often plays tennis at □ □ often plays tennis on
   plays often tennis on □ □ plays often tennis at

9 We haven't got a record-player. Let's _____ .
   lend Mary's one □ □ to borrow the Mary's
   to lend one of Mary □ □ borrow Mary's

10 I'd like to leave my car near here. Where's the _____ , please?
   nearest car park □ □ nearest parking
   next car park □ □ next parking

11 I _____ abroad next week.
   going to □ □ am going
   shall be go □ □ will be go

12 If I _____ working immediately, it would have been all right.
   had stopped □ □ would stop
   stopped □ □ would have stopped

13 I _____ send you to hospital for an X-ray. Here's the note for the hospital.
   would like to □ □ will like to
   would □ □ am wanting to

14 He told me that he _____ in Naples for the previous year.
   has been working □ □ has worked
   had been worked □ □ had been working

15 When I answered the phone, my girlfriend _____ 'hello'.
   said □ □ was telling
   was saying □ □ told

16 I've brought you _____ flowers for your birthday.
   few □ □ a few
   a little □ □ little

17 He didn't know _____ or stay at home.
   if to go □ □ to go
   whether to go □ □ if that he should go

18 Don't wait for me if you _____ .
   have speed □ □ are in a speed
   have a hurry □ □ are in a hurry

19 Who is responsible _____ the arrangements?
   for make □ □ to make
   to making □ □ for making

20 He works too hard. That is _____ is wrong with him.
   that which □ □ the what
   what □ □ the thing what

21 They'll hurt _____ if we don't stop them fighting.
   each other □ □ each the other
   one the other □ □ one to another

22 He is _____ to come home early this evening.
   probable □ □ likely
   probably □ □ may be

23 I know it's not important but I can't help _____ about it.
   to think □ □ think
   thinking □ □ except to think

24 I learnt how to _____ a bicycle when I was six years old.
   ride □ □ drive
   conduct □ □ lead

25 They _____ on holiday in Switzerland and became good friends.
   found □ □ knew
   met □ □ encountered

Name and date

Quickcheck Test D2

A Nelson Copy Master   © W S Fowler and Norman Coe 1987

Example:

This _____ a book.
- is ■
- am ☐
- are ☐
- be ☐

In each question, only one of the four answers is correct. Choose the correct answer and fill in the square next to it. Fill in only one square for each question. The example shows you what to do.

D3

1. They live _____ the other side of the road.
   - in ☐
   - on ☐
   - for ☐
   - by ☐

2. I should have asked her for a plan of the house. If I _____ I would have found everything.
   - did ☐
   - would ☐
   - have ☐
   - had ☐

3. When my wife _____ back tomorrow, she'll find everything in order.
   - will come ☐
   - shall come ☐
   - comes ☐
   - come ☐

4. After _____ information without success, we bought a book on the subject.
   - asking ☐
   - to ask ☐
   - to ask for ☐
   - asking for ☐

5. He's _____ his sister.
   - much more tall that ☐
   - much more tall than ☐
   - much taller than ☐
   - much taller that ☐

6. She had three sons, all _____ became doctors.
   - of whom ☐
   - who ☐
   - which ☐
   - of which ☐

7. He made me _____ .
   - that I got angry ☐
   - be angry ☐
   - to be angry ☐
   - angry ☐

8. We usually have fine weather _____ summer.
   - in ☐
   - while ☐
   - at ☐
   - on ☐

9. _____ of them understood him.
   - Anyone ☐
   - Someone ☐
   - No one ☐
   - None ☐

10. That's the firm _____ .
    - we've been dealing with ☐
    - what we've been treating with ☐
    - what we've been dealing with ☐
    - we've been treating with ☐

11. He isn't _____ to reach the ceiling.
    - enough tall ☐
    - tall enough ☐
    - so tall ☐
    - as tall ☐

12. He'd done that before, _____ ?
    - hadn't he ☐
    - didn't he ☐
    - shouldn't he ☐
    - wouldn't he ☐

13. She let the children _____ to play.
    - go out ☐
    - to go out ☐
    - that they went out ☐
    - going out ☐

14. I'm going to spend a few days with some _____ of mine, who live in the north of Scotland.
    - companies ☐
    - neighbours ☐
    - familiars ☐
    - relatives ☐

15. I didn't write it. That isn't my _____ on the cheque.
    - signature ☐
    - letter ☐
    - firm ☐
    - mark ☐

16. We arrived _____ England a week ago.
    - to ☐
    - in ☐
    - on ☐
    - at ☐

17. He paid _____ in five-pound notes.
    - how much the car ☐
    - the car for ☐
    - for the car ☐
    - the car ☐

18. The office is only _____ from here.
    - at 100 yards away ☐
    - at 100 yards far ☐
    - about 100 yards far ☐
    - about 100 yards away ☐

19. _____ problem for foreigners remembering to drive on the left.
    - It's so much ☐
    - That's so much ☐
    - That's such a ☐
    - It's such a ☐

20. We'll have to drive carefully _____ home.
    - on the way to ☐
    - in the way ☐
    - on the way ☐
    - in the way to ☐

21. I told them how to get here but perhaps I _____ them a map.
    - should have given ☐
    - ought give ☐
    - had to give ☐
    - must have given ☐

22. What a nuisance! I _____ to all this trouble if I'd known they weren't coming.
    - mustn't have gone ☐
    - needn't have gone ☐
    - didn't need to go ☐
    - hadn't to go ☐

23. He won the first _____ in the competition.
    - reward ☐
    - premium ☐
    - prize ☐
    - price ☐

24. Sixty per cent of television viewers chose him as their _____ actor.
    - favourite ☐
    - preferred ☐
    - popular ☐
    - favoured ☐

25. They're staying with us _____ the time being until they find a place of their own.
    - in ☐
    - since ☐
    - for ☐
    - during ☐

Name and date

Quickcheck Test D3

Example:

This _____ a book.
- is ■
- am ☐
- are ☐
- be ☐

In each question, only one of the four answers is correct. Choose the correct answer and fill in the square next to it. Fill in only one square for each question. The example shows you what to do.

D4

1 Sometimes _____ gets on the bus and checks the tickets.
- an agent ☐
- an inspector ☐
- a conductor ☐
- an officer ☐

2 He'll soon get _____ his disappointment and be quite cheerful again by the morning.
- away ☐
- through ☐
- out of ☐
- over ☐

3 You'll soon get used to his ways, _____ everyone else.
- as ☐
- similar than ☐
- like ☐
- the same that ☐

4 He lives on a farm, _____ the castle.
- quite near at ☐
- nearby to ☐
- not much far from ☐
- not far away from ☐

5 The little man was _____ one metre fifty high.
- nearly more than ☐
- just as much as ☐
- hardly more than ☐
- almost more than ☐

6 I'll take down your name and address in case you _____ as a witness.
- are needed ☐
- will be needed ☐
- need ☐
- will need ☐

7 The car he was driving _____ .
- can have been robbed ☐
- may have been robbed ☐
- can have been stolen ☐
- may have been stolen ☐

8 _____ you're happy, it doesn't matter if you haven't got much money.
- As long as ☐
- During ☐
- Meanwhile ☐
- As far as ☐

9 He used to wait for me, _____ together.
- for walking home ☐
- for walking to home ☐
- so that we could walk to home ☐
- so that we could walk home ☐

10 Steak pie! That's my favourite _____ .
- dish ☐
- menu ☐
- plate ☐
- receipt ☐

11 He asked me what was _____ in the street outside.
- succeeding ☐
- going on ☐
- doing up ☐
- making out ☐

12 We were _____ for half an hour in the traffic and so we arrived late.
- held up ☐
- kept off ☐
- broken down ☐
- put back ☐

13 He worked in those terrible conditions for _____ he could stand it.
- as long as ☐
- so long as ☐
- as far as ☐
- so far as ☐

14 The ship was _____ danger of sinking.
- with ☐
- under ☐
- on ☐
- in ☐

15 It took _____ to repair the boat.
- an hour's work ☐
- the work of an hour ☐
- a work hour ☐
- an hour work ☐

16 They succeeded _____ the mud.
- in disposing ☐
- in getting rid of ☐
- to remove ☐
- to take off ☐

17 He's a nice dog. He won't do you any _____ .
- bite ☐
- ill ☐
- harm ☐
- hurt ☐

18 There's no beer left and the pubs are shut so you'll have to _____ .
- go off ☐
- go for ☐
- go through ☐
- go without ☐

19 She's such an irritating woman. I don't know how you can _____ her.
- put up ☐
- stand with ☐
- stand up with ☐
- put up with ☐

20 The good service at the hotel _____ the poor food to some extent.
- made up ☐
- made out ☐
- made up for ☐
- made for ☐

21 I _____ of the way he behaved at the meeting.
- disapproved ☐
- disagreed ☐
- condemned ☐
- objected ☐

22 He is looking for a job that will give him greater _____ for using his own initiative.
- suitability ☐
- scope ☐
- space ☐
- place ☐

23 The country needs a _____ government. We have had three Prime Ministers in a year.
- stationary ☐
- changeless ☐
- stable ☐
- constant ☐

24 It was dark in the tunnel so he _____ a match.
- struck ☐
- burnt ☐
- hit ☐
- fired ☐

25 I will never _____ them to take the child away from me.
- admit ☐
- tolerate ☐
- allow ☐
- let ☐

Name and date

Quickcheck Test D4

A Nelson Copy Master   © W S Fowler and Norman Coe 1987